Bayerische
Schlösserverwaltung
The Bavarian Administration
of State Castles

Neuschwanstein

Peter O. Krückmann

Prestel
Munich · London · New York

Contents

Foreword 7

Building 'The Castle of the Holy Grail' 9

A Tour of Neuschwanstein 14

    The Courtyards 14
    The Royal Residence 15
    The Throne Room 18
    The Lower Anteroom 24
    The King's Apartments 26
    The Dining Room 27
    The Bedroom 29
    The Dressing Room 34
    The Living Room 35
    The Venus Grotto and Winter Garden 38
    The Study 39
    The Upper Anteroom 44
    The Singers' Hall 48
    The Kitchen 54

Traditional but Modern 56

Embroidered curtain from the bedroom

following pages:
The castles Neuschwanstein and Hohenschwangau in front of Lake Alp and the Schlicken mountains

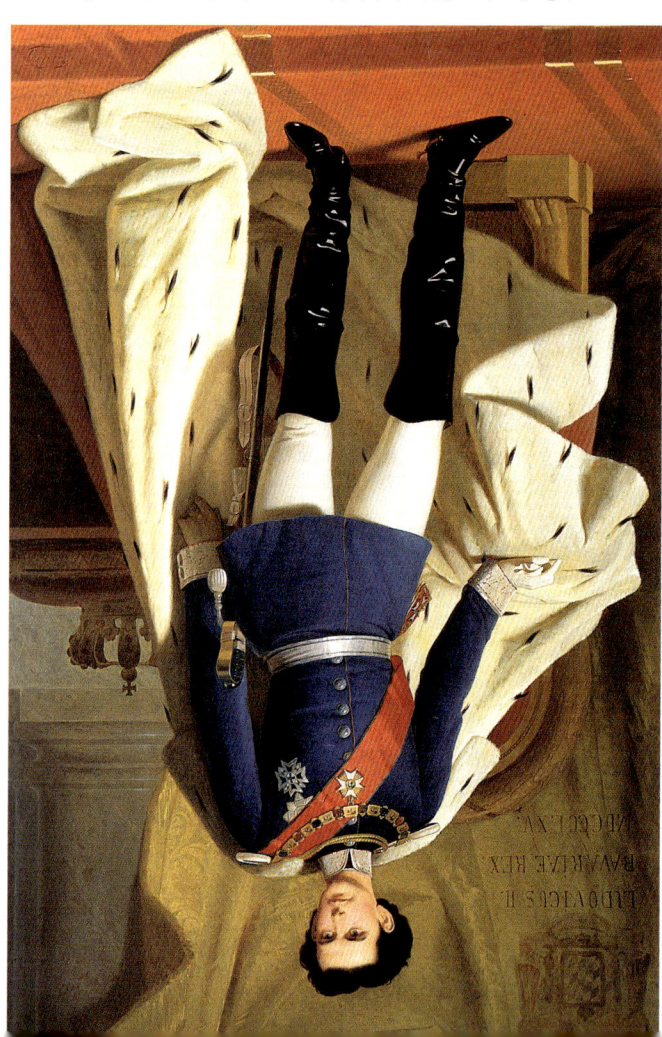

Ferdinand von Piloty, Ludwig II in a general's uniform and coronation vestments, 1865 (Ludwig II Museum at Herrenchiemsee)

Ferdinand Leeke, A Genius Crowns Ludwig II, c. 1887 (Ludwig II Museum at Herrenchiemsee)

FOREWORD

Although he was born more than a century and a half ago and died in 1888, aged just 41, King Ludwig II of Bavaria is anything but a dusty figure from the moth-ridden attic of history. Together with only a few other personalities in history, the Bavarian monarch has attained a degree of popularity which must fill the hearts of many modern entertainment industry stars with envy. Since his fans have even gone so far as making him the hero of a musical, the fairy-tale king's canonization and acceptance into the heaven of immortals is complete. By building a musical theater at an exposed location not far from the mountain on which the castle is located, his admirers have now consecrated a shrine to the king who, in his time, had constructed Neuschwanstein as a temple for glorifying the Holy Grail. In the meantime, Ludwig's most famous castle has itself achieved the status of a pop icon as the subject of a series of prints by Andy Warhol. This, however, is only one aspect of the "Ludwig Phenomenon." The other side of his story is incongruously serious. It has to do with the thoroughly tragic person of the king who subordinated his entire existence as a human being and monarch to his striving for the sublime—whatever he understood that to be—and who, in his own way, realized vast projects that continue to fill millions of visitors with wonder, while at the same time, his own life was doomed to failure.

Throughout his life Ludwig felt harried

Foreword

Christian Jank, draft for the Upper Court, 1871 (Ludwig II Museum at Herrenchiemsee, Wittelsbacher Ausgleichsfond)

by challenges of various kinds: from his parents with whom he had so little in common, from teachers who tried to change him, from his tortured homoerotic inclination which gave him the deepest pangs of conscience, as well as from a narrow-minded administration apparatus and political disappointments, brought by the founding of the Reich in 1870 which questioned Bavarian sovereignty. All of this made his interest in the daily matters of state fade away, alienating him more and more from the people around him. Surrounded by an environment which humiliated and misunderstood him, the king withdrew into the solitude of the lower Alpine region in Bavaria, where he created his own cosmos and could live protected from the harshness of the outside world.

Building 'The Castle of the Holy Grail'

Things just couldn't be done fast enough. In 1868, only four years after his coronation, the twenty-three year old King Ludwig II ordered the drafting of plans for a castle to be built within view of his parents' seat Hohenschwangau. The theater scene-painter Ch. Jank created fanciful designs; E. Riedel transformed them into architectural plans; G. Dollmann continued the work as of 1874. The cornerstone was already laid in 1869. Construction began with a gatehouse. Inside, an apartment for the King was created from which he could observe the progress being made. Recalling impressions from his youth at Hohenschwangau, as well as being inspired by Wartburg Castle which he had visited in 1867, Ludwig attempted to revive the tradition of medieval chivalry in his plans for Neuschwanstein. Starting with the original idea of a small building of almost playful lightness with many picturesque details, a plan soon grew for a monumental castle in a neo-Romanesque style. In 1880, the basic structure of Neuschwanstein, which is at the same time a fortress and a royal residence, had been finished; the entire complex however was only completed in a simplified form in 1892, after the king's death. Only the principle rooms in the castle would be furnished during Ludwig II's lifetime. The mural painters W. Hauschild, E. Schwoiser, A. Spieß, F. von Piloty, E. Ille, and J. Aigner, who are

Christian Jank, preliminary draft for Neuschwanstein castle, 1868 (Ludwig II Museum at Herrenchiemsee, Wittelsbacher Ausgleichsfond)

Building 'The Castle of the Holy Grail'

barely known today, created a walk-through picture book depicting mythical scenes from the Middle Ages in Germany, scenes now so foreign to us today. Since these murals are not considered to be truly exceptional from an artistic point of view, the following guided tour will not devote attention to a closer examination of the contributions made by particular artists. From many of Ludwig's comments we can conclude that, in fact, the rapid execution of the works to his specific instructions was more important than any artistic considerations.

Those who visit Neuschwanstein with overly romantic expectations will perhaps be surprised by the castle's almost sober character. Ludwig wanted it that way since, according to him, all false ornamentation would contradict the dignity of the building. But this also goes to prove that Neuschwanstein is a modern building. Modern too was the engineering technology which made it possible for work on Neuschwanstein to be completed within the tight deadlines set by the king. Not to mention the necessity of first building a road up the 200 meter-high mountain, of preparing the ground for the foundations using dynamite to remove the ruins of a medieval structure and to blast away the rock, or of providing the building site with a new water supply. The transport of enormous masses of building materials up the mountain posed serious logistic prob-

Neuschwanstein as seen from the south, state of construction by November 1881, photograph by Ludwig Schradler and son, Füssen

10

Building 'The Castle of the Holy Grail'

lems. The builders met this challenge with the most modern technology available by installing a steam crane held by wooden scaffolding on the west side, one of the first machines of this type to be used in Germany.

Seen from an art-historical point of view, Neuschwanstein is recognized as one of the most important examples of Historicism. But for tourists traveling to it from all over the world, this castle, perched imposingly on a steep rock outcrop, seems quintessentially medieval. It is rewarding to pause and think about how this came to be, and why Neuschwanstein just seems like a figment of our imagination, or a magic spell summoning a long-gone era.

Originally Neuschwanstein was intended as a temple' to Richard Wagner. *Tristan and Isolde*, *Lohengrin*, *Tannhäuser*, and *Die Meistersinger* were the operas from which the motifs for the murals were supposed to be taken. The Lord of the Castle, however, finally ordered that the decoration of the rooms should not be based on the operas themselves, but on the original sagas. In that way Ludwig hoped to avoid making the rooms seem to be mere illustrations of the operas composed by his fatherly friend. Even if many of Wagner's ideas still influenced the painting of the

Neuschwanstein's state of construction at the time of King Ludwig II's death, 1886, illustration by Ludwig Assmus

Building 'The Castle of the Holy Grail'

The castle as seen from the north, with corner tower, knights' house and royal residence.

murals and, even if Ludwig could hardly see the sagas other than as they appeared filtered through the Wagnerian texts, something else mattered too. With Neuschwanstein he envisioned resurrecting Mont Salvat, the mythical castle of the Holy Grail in the land Salvatterra where the knights kept the holy cup which Christ used at the Last Supper, and in which Joseph of Aramathia collected the blood of the crucified savior. For him the world of the Grail was the most chivalrous and exalted form of Christian endeavor. Recent art-historical research has only now been able to clarify how such notions can be explained solely on the basis of Ludwig's own life history. The gravely oppressive conflict he endured between a guilt-ridden eroticism, with which he struggled throughout his life, and his resultant deep longing for purity and holiness, weighed heavily upon him. Sin and salvation are the basic concepts on which the legends to be illustrated were chosen.

Approaching from the north, from Schwangau, or from the pilgrimage church Wies, Neuschwanstein castle slowly takes on clear contours among the wooded slopes under the rugged rock face of the Säuling—an impressive sight. Only when we come much closer do we realize that Neuschwanstein is built on a rock outcrop, and that the structure is of a massiveness which we at first hardly believe to be possible. First designs, when the building was still intended to be of more modest dimensions, already show that the location and form of Neuschwanstein were consciously staged for the benefit of the viewer. The extent to which the castle was designed to be looked at—and for Ludwig that meant to be meditated over in its symbolism as the Grail mountain—becomes only fully apparent by walking along the high path on the Säuling. Several different vantage points offer new, impressive views of the castle, especially when it is seen with Hohenschwangau and the Alpsee (Lake Alp) in the background.

A highpoint of the guided route is the daring steel construction of Marienbrücke (Mary's Bridge) over the seemingly bottomless Pöllatschlucht (Pöllat Gorge), a masterful combination of a filigree technical structure in harmony with the surrounding nature.

Marienbrücke (Mary's Bridge) across the Pöllat Gorge

Building 'The Castle of the Holy Grail'

13

A TOUR OF NEUSCHWANSTEIN

The Courtyards

A long drive winds up to the crenelated gatehouse flanked by corner towers. Behind it, first the lower, then, above that, the upper courts, are surprisingly spacious. A 90-meter-high tower was originally planned to be built in the latter. On the ground level a Gothic chapel was to be built—its outline is indicated by the paving in the courtyard. Surrounding the courtyard, to the north and opposite the living quarters, is the knights' house, and towering above

The Upper Court with the living quarters, royal residence, knights' house and corner tower

everything is the main building, the royal residence, comprising the state apartments, the throne room, and the singers' hall.

The Royal Residence

The ground floor comprises the kitchen and other service rooms, and the first floor above ground-level was reserved for servants. The next floor above was supposed to contain rooms for guests, in particular Richard Wagner, whom the king expected to stay for long

Wilhelm Hauschild, *St. Klothilde Converts Her Husband to Christianity*, 1886, mural in the throne room

periods at a time. Once their relationship had cooled over the course of time and the king had become increasingly unsociable, its completion was no longer necessary. Here the unfinished structure affords an insight into the often surprising technology involved in the construction which combines steel girders and masonry faced with limestone. Today the visitors' center is located in this part of the castle. The third floor above ground-level can be reached by a spiral staircase giving access to the king's private living quarters east of the forecourt and the majestic throne room opposite.

The Throne Room

In a certain sense the apotheosis—the transfiguration of the king who longed for salvation—takes place in the mighty throne room on the opposite side of the castle. After passing along the winding route through many rooms and past many staircases, the visitor is stunned by the cool, gold-shimmering opulence and bright light of this unexpectedly spacious room. Suddenly it is as though one has entered a Byzantine church. The structure was modeled on the Hagia Sophia in Istanbul, as well as on the historicist palace church of All Saints in the royal residence in Munich.

A star-covered dome reaches up from walls articulated by rows of columns of stuccoed lapis lazuli and porphyry, with aisles beyond. In contrast to the

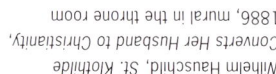

preceding pages:
The throne room

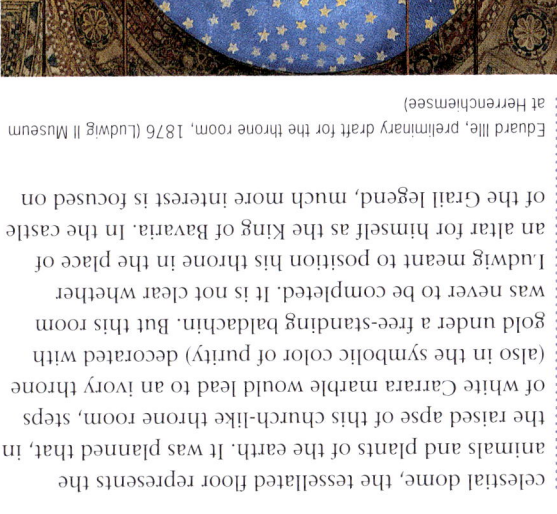

Eduard Ille, preliminary draft for the throne room, 1876 (Ludwig II Museum at Herrenchiemsee)

celestial dome, the tessellated floor represents the animals and plants of the earth. It was planned that, in the raised apse of this church-like throne room, steps of white Carrara marble would lead to an ivory throne (also in the symbolic color of purity) decorated with gold under a free-standing baldachin. But this room was never to be completed. It is not clear whether Ludwig meant to position his throne in the place of an altar for himself as the King of Bavaria. In the castle of the Grail legend, much more interest is focused on

left: Anton Spenger, draft for the tessellated floor in the throne room (Ludwig II Museum at Herrenchiemsee)

right:
Waldemar Kolmsperger, *St. George Slaying the Dragon*, 1884, mural on the rear wall in the throne room

"the unknown king of the Grail" for whose arrival the room was constructed. Today it is an accepted fact that Ludwig secretly identified with the latter in his fantasy world. We can conclude this from the iconographic scenes in the room, which Ludwig personally worked out in great detail. Passages from his descriptions of the murals, which reveal so much about his way of thinking, are quoted here in translation:

Corresponding ... to the exalted purpose of the throne room, the images found within it are chosen in order to point out the throne as the source of authoritative legislation.

In order to illustrate this, the lawmakers of the great heathen civilized nations are shown in the large, shield-shaped fields of the dome to the left of the throne: Manu representing the Indians, Zoroaster the Persians, Hermes the Egyptians, Solon the Greeks, and Augustus representing the world-dominating Romans.

On the right is Moses, who received the laws revealed by God.

Opposite the throne are the three Magi, the wise men from the Orient who followed the star, the symbol of the divine light which was shed upon the world.

Under this portrait are St. Michael, as the victor over spiritual evil, and St. George as the conqueror of the forces of physical evil.

Tour of the castle

Wilhelm Hauschild, *Christ in Glory and Canonized kings*, 1886, mural in the apse of the throne room

The niche in the throne shows Christ, the supreme law-maker, sitting on the rainbow and surrounded by cherubim and the symbolic attributes of the Evangelists, as a sign that he is ruler over heaven and earth.

At his feet kneel St. Mary and John the Baptist, as intercessors for mankind ... Angels, praying, are on both sides.

Above the throne stand six holy kings, paragons, who shine under palms of peace, for their fulfilling and guarding of the divine laws.

Near the steps to the throne, on the side walls, stand the twelve holy Apostles, as the champions of the divine commandments.

Tour of the castle

On the walls of the room, the eminent traits of character from the lives of the six holy kings are represented.

Above and to the right of the throne [on the gallery]:
St. Stephan, King of Hungary, striving to guide the heathen Hungarians towards Christianity.

Thereupon: St. Heinrich of Germany and Roman Emperor, who builds churches and monasteries in reverence of God and who introduces solicitous friars to serve God and multiply his people.

Above and to the left of the throne: St. Louis, King of France, with considerable condescension, feeding and clothing the poor.

To the right of the throne at the bottom [in the arcades]:
St. Edward, King of England, protecting the rights of all subjects as the righteous knight on the throne.

St. Ferdinand, King of Spain, fights the enemies of Christianity with heroic valor.

On the left of the throne at the bottom: St. Casimir, Prince of Poland, devoting himself to piety in quiet retreat.

[On the left in the arcades]: Portrayed as representatives of the female virtues are St. Clotilde, Queen of France, teaching her heathen husband about Christianity, and St. Elisabeth, Marchioness of Thuringia, nursing the poor and sick.

Placing the symbolic signs of the seven gifts of the Holy Ghost on the arch encircling the throne indicates that true legislation and compliance with the law can be found in such works.

From this description it becomes clear how Ludwig himself saw his role as king, namely as following in the tradition of those kings who created an eternal realm of peace, a Golden Age on earth, through their "fulfillment ... of the divine laws"—a gigantic demand to which only a gigantic room could do justice. At the same time, it also reveals a fantasy of greatness which surely can be understood as a form of compensation for the humiliations suffered in his youth. On the other hand, through this idealization—indeed transfiguration—of kingship, Ludwig himself engaged in a destructively tense conflict. Because of his homosexuality, he considered himself unworthy of his office. Of course his attitude was also irreconcilable with the

actual political circumstances of his time. As a constitutional monarch he could by no means fulfill his claim to "authoritative law-making." A dream of rulership such as that reflected in the scenes in the throne room was unrealizable by any stretch of the imagination. In fact, Ludwig never had the intention of carrying out any acts of state in the throne room. It served his dreams alone. Only in his fantasies could Ludwig experience himself as that Byzantine ruler, as a holy knight and identify with the St. George on the mural, boldly slaying the dragon. Through the decoration on his helmet he is shown to be the swan knight and lord of the castle Neuschwanstein, in other words, as King Ludwig himself. In the background the castle is depicted perched high on a rocky outcrop.

The Lower Anteroom

The Sigurd Saga of the Eddas, which in many respects corresponds to the Siegfried Saga from *The King of the*

The lower anteroom with murals by Ferdinand von Piloty and other artists

Nibelung, unfolds on the walls of the anteroom between the throne room and the royal apartments.

To the past history of the saga: One evening, on their wanderings through the world, the gods Odin, Häner and Loke kill an otter which was just consuming a salmon. It turns out that the otter was in fact the son of the wizard Hreidmar. Regin and Fafnir are also brothers of the otter. In order to atone for this bloody act, Loke, who committed the deed, has to supply enough gold to completely cover the flayed skin of the otter. Loke extorts the gold from the dwarf Andwari from the ancient family of the Nibelung's. Out of greed he also demands his ring upon which the dwarf lays a curse. The ring soon produces its effect when Fafnir and Regin slay their father, so that they alone can own the treasure of gold. Fafnir denies his brother his share and expels him form his village. Now the sole owner of the treasure, Fafnir transforms into a dragon and lies down on top of the gold. The brother on the other hand settles as a smith close to the cave.

The cycle begins on the right wall, as the young Sigurd hears the prophecy of his destiny.

Sigurd then comes to Regin, who wants to use the young knight as his avenger. In the second picture, Regin forges a sword for Sigurd that is so sharp that it can easily split his anvil.

With it, Sigurd is to slay Regin's brother, Fafnir, in order to reach the treasure of the Nibelung, which can be seen in the following image. A gigantic dragon rears up in front of him. After he has bathed in its blood, Sigurd understands the language of the birds, who warn him of Regin's perfidy. Thereupon he kills Regin as well, and thus gains possession of the cursed treasure.

Further on his way he finds Brunhild sleeping in a ring of fire, into which Odin has banished her. Brunhild belongs to the Valkyries, who serve the fallen heroes gathered in Odin's golden palace Valhalla, after they have chosen those who will die in battle—as the translation of their name expresses. Captured by her beauty, he swears eternal loyalty to her.

Sigurd then rides on and reaches the court of the King of the Franks where—in the image above the window—he meets the king's daughter, Gudrun. With a magic potion she makes him forget his oath, whereupon Sigurd takes her as his wife.

With Gudrun's brother, Gjukinger, Sigurd travels to Atli, King of the Huns, to win his sister, Brunhild, as a wife for Gunnar, another brother of Gudrun's. Sigurd accomplishes this goal with an insidious ruse. On the left wall the story continues with Sigurd's murder, on the order of the abandoned Brunhild, during his rest in a forest clearing.

The next painting shows Gudrun, waiting in vain for Sigurd while, in the final painting, Brunhild mocks Gudrun's brother and her husband Gunnar, telling him that she was never in love with him, but with Sigurd.

On the entrance wall, Gudrun mourns at the body of Sigurd and, in the next painting, Sigurd and Brunhild are burned and thus united in death.

Like many other picture cycles in Neuschwanstein, the Sigurd Saga is a commentary on Ludwig's conviction that, because of conflicting passions, true love cannot be achieved on earth but only in a spiritual form in the afterlife. The saga is continued in the upper anteroom beyond the king's apartment.

The King's Apartments

The king's apartments can be entered from the anteroom by passing through a servant's room and then the dining room. Like almost all other rooms of the apartments, it is furnished for the most part with artistically carved oak paneling in Romanesque forms. On the upper wall surfaces, space is left for paintings, many of which were done on rough canvas in order to imitate tapestry. Particularly precious are the curtains and upholstery fabrics, some of which are now stored in a depot for conservation reasons. Accents are set by tiled stoves of varying shapes.

The Dining Room

In the dining room, the visitor is introduced to the world of the *Minnesang* at the court of Count Hermann of Thuringia. Over the doors, the portraits of the famous singers Gottfried von Strassburg, Wolfram von Eschenbach,

Ludwig Bierling and Eduard Wollenweber, Siegfried *Slaying the Dragon*, 1885/86, gold-plated bronze sculpture in the dining room

Joseph Aigner, *The War of the Singers at Wartburg*, 1886, mural in the dining room

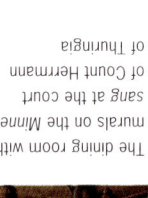

The dining room with murals on the Minnesang at the court of Count Herrmann of Thuringia

and Reinmar von Zweter can be seen. The message here picks up on the theme of the Sigurd Saga. The actual theme of the minnesingers' poems is alluded to here: the pure—as opposed to the physical—love of a woman. The ulterior meaning is that of the Virgin Mary transposed into the worldly realm. The love poems sung by the minnesingers also stand for the conquest over all that is "evil and base" in mankind, represented here by the elaborate bronze sculpture *Siegfried Slaying the Dragon* on the dining room table. In all this, Ludwig created a monument to himself.

The Bedroom

In the next room, the bedroom, and in the small chapel adjacent, there is a change of styles to the Gothic. Delicately carved wooden spires and tracery work decorate the bed—lending it the appearance of a cathedral, the washing stand with the water spout in the shape of a swan, the throne-like reading chair, and indeed the entire wall paneling. This interplay with artistic styles is not an expression of the master's whim. The king was quite consciously trying to make a meaningful statement. The Romanesque period, which otherwise characterizes the entire castle, was supposed to allude to the ancient origins of the legends. The Gothic style, on the other hand, in imitation of nineteenth-century reconstructions of the temple of the Grail which were very familiar to Ludwig, appears holy and exalted. For Ludwig, the bedroom was by no means a place of intimate pleasure, but should rather be understood as a type of monk's cell—albeit one splendid enough for a king. The denial of sensuality is also the theme of the painted scenes from Gottfried von Strassburg's *Tristan*, a tale in many aspects similar to the legend of Sigurd.

During a single combat on an adventurous trip to Ireland, Tristan, the son of King Meliadus, is seriously wounded and nursed back to health by Isolde with magic herbs. Later he arrives at the court of King Mark

Wilhelm Hauschild,
St. Louis, 1880/81,
altarpiece in the house
chapel

in Cornwall, his
father's brother-
in-law. He sends
him back to Isolde
to win her as the
king's wife, which
he manages to do.
This is where the
Tristan and Isolde
cycle begins to the
right of the tiled
stove.

On the passage back—it is calm and sultry—Tristan and
Isolde drink a cup of wine, unaware that it is a love potion
intended for the old king Mark.

The image on the rear wall of the room shows the two,
now inflamed with love, as they secretly meet in the
garden of the king's castle, even though Isolde has in
the meantime married king Mark. It is framed by allegor-
ical figures of loyalty and courtly love.

King Mark hears about the love affair and sentences
Tristan to death, who then manages to flee. In the
picture to the right of the bed, Isolde gives Tristan a
ring as a symbol of her love and loyalty as he takes his
leave.

At the castle of King Hoel in Brittany, Tristan longingly
awaits the arrival of Isolde's ship, depicted in the next
picture. King Mark, who has learned that it was a magic
potion, which had kindled the love between the two,
and who forgives them for their involuntary infidelity,
accompanies his wife.

*preceding
pages*:
Bedroom
with *Tristan
and Isolde*
mural

Above the reading chair, the series of images ends with
the death of the lovers. While Tristan dies of exhaustion
and longing, Isolde succumbs to grief.

Tour of the castle

Figures of the lovers decorate the tiled stove which stands between the beginning and the end of the story.
From his reading chair, Ludwig could contemplate a paragon representing the conquering of earthly passions and salvation in holiness. The altar painting in the house chapel, bathed in the mystical light of the stained glass window, depicts a saint who shares the king's name—Saint Louis IX of France.

The dressing room with murals depicting the lives and works of Hans Sachs and Walther von der Vogelweide

Embroidered curtain in the dressing room

The Dressing Room

The next room, the comparatively simple dressing room, is decorated with motifs from the lives and works of Walther von der Vogelweide and Hans Sachs. Thus, the middle of the stove wall shows the shoe-maker-cum-poet as he sings a new song for Nuremberg artists and humanists; below them to the left are the ore-foundry owner Peter Vischer and Willibald Pirkhei-mer, the famous scholar and friend of Albrecht Dürer, who stands to the right of Sachs. The emperor Maximi-lian can be seen at the edge of the picture. The central painting is flanked by an image of the journeyman Walther riding away, and a reference to his famous poem: "Ich saz auf einem steine ..." (I sat on a stone). Note the painted sky, which alludes to the theme of nature in the poetry of Walther von der Vogelweide.

Tour of the castle

The Living Room

Beyond the dressing room lies the spacious living room, which is divided by an archway. Its decoration is devoted to the saga of Lohengrin.

Like a colophon, the swan knight, with whom Ludwig identified throughout his life, is painted to resemble a Gobelin on the northern wall opposite the entrance. As the son of Parsifal, he was predestined to a life as a knight of the Grail.

August von Heckel, *Lohengrin's Arrival in Brabant* (detail), mural in the living room

The so-called miracle of the Grail, the Grail's election of Lohengrin as the protector of Elsa, an imperiled princess from Brabant, is shown in the large-format painting opposite.

Next to it over the door, Lohengrin is once again seated in the boat drawn by a swan.

The knight of the Grail must now fight hand-to-hand with Telramund, and is victorious. Then Lohengrin and Elsa marry. This is depicted on the walls of the alcove.

A condition for their union, however, was that Elsa never seek to inquire as to her husband's name and family. Yet, in arrogant fear that Lohengrin might indeed be socially

The living room with the "miracle of the Grail" from the Lohengrin saga

below her, she asks the fateful question. This scene is shown on the wall to the right of the alcove, while over the door on the right we see how Lohengrin thereupon leaves with the swan to return to the castle of the Grail.

When Ludwig sat on the bench below the illustration of the miracle of the Grail, with a table next to him covered by an embroidered cloth bearing the image of a swan—the leitmotif of Neuschwanstein—he could imagine himself as the swan knight. In him, he found

Tour of the castle

his own paragon of purity, a mythological model of a selfless existence in the service of the most exalted values.

The Venus Grotto and Winter Garden

The passageway leading off the living room comes as a surprise, for here—on the third floor above ground-level—the king had a small grotto constructed, an allusion to the Venus grotto which appears again in painted form in the last of the king's rooms, the study. The grotto is also an antechamber to a winter garden. The contrast between the "underground" area enclosed by stone and the following open-air environment is striking.

There, in the artificial dripstone cavern, a magical atmosphere was created by colored electric light, and a small waterfall. Here Ludwig could feel carried away in an illusionary world with tropical plants. The three-meter-high panes of sheet glass—at that time the largest single panes of glass produced in Germany—truly give the impression of being outside.

The Venus Grotto

Tour of the castle

The winter garden with a view over the low-lying country to the north

The Study

Like all of the king's seating arrangements and tables in Neuschwanstein, the writing desk in the study did not primarily fulfill practical needs. It was much rather a place for him to contemplate his own life, salvation from earthly sin, and the images all around him

Tour of the castle

Philipp Perrons and Ferdinand Harrach, writing set with the figure of Lohengrin

showing heroes of past epochs who faced similar challenges. Even his writing pen bears the figure of Lohengrin, the swan knight of the Holy Grail, and the murals around the room depict the tragic life of Tannhäuser, a minstrel whose life can be seen as an allegory for Ludwig's own human struggles.

The illustrations begin at the far end of the right wall where Tannhäuser is seated at the feet of Lady Venus and her companions in the cavern of the Hörsel Mountain—a telling symbol that he has succumbed to physical love. His pensive pose suggests that he has nonetheless grown tired of being with the goddess of feminine sensuality. For courtly love aspires to the ideal of pure, spiritual love.

preceding pages:
Study with *Tannhäuser in the Venus Grotto*

He flees from this world and starts off for the war of the minstrels at Wartburg Castle. This, and his arrival there, are shown in the pictures over the passageway doors.

His repentance is still weak, however, for once again he sings to the glory of erotic love, much to the dismay of the gathered knights—this is shown on the large mural over the tiled stove.

The painting on the rear wall to the right shows his execration by the pope, to whom he then makes a pilgrimage—but in vain.

The rear wall of the archway shows how Tannhäuser returns to the Venus mountain, resigned and unredeemed.

Joseph Aigner, *Tannhäuser Setting out for Wartburg*, 1880/81, mural in the study

The Upper Anteroom

Returning to the antechamber and climbing the spiral
staircase, the visitor reaches the fourth story where the
impressive singers' hall is located above the king's living quarters. The newel post at the end of the staircase
is in the shape of a palm tree reaching up into a starry

Tour of the castle

View from the balcony of the throne room over Lake Alp and Hohenschwangau

sky. Ludwig, who consciously planned every element, found a pictorial means to transform this act of climbing into a symbol of the striving for transcendence from an imperfect life on earth, into an eternal, divine realm.

The murals in the upper anteroom are the continuation of the cycle seen in the lower anteroom with the Gudrun saga by the elder Edda.

Again, the story begins on the right wall, as the mourning Gudrun withdraws to her sister Thora after the death of Sigurd and embroiders the heroic deeds of her ancestors on a tapestry—the subject of the second painting.

The two following pictures show three kings asking for her hand, including King Atli from Hunnaland, and her journey is depicted as a bridge to his castle. Atli is less interested in her than in the treasure of the Nibelung's, which has been in possession of her family since Sigurd's death. Together with the treasure is the fateful ring, whose deadly curse is soon to show its effect.

right: The top of the spiral staircase on the fourth floor above ground level

Wilhelm Hauschild, *Gudrun Welcoming Gunnar and Högni*, 1883/84, mural in the upper anteroom

Tour of the castle

On the window wall we see Atli, who is telling Gudrun of his dreams of battle turmoil.

The continuation of the story on the left wall shows the messengers of Atli—who finally wants to get hold of the Nibelung booty—presenting Atli's invitation to Gunnar and his brother Högni.

In the following painting above the door, Gunnar and Högni arrive at Atli's court, where they are greeted by their sister. Suspecting Atli's intention, they sink the treasure in the Rhine.

This is followed by the Huns attacking their guests and the funeral banquet which Gudrun then holds for the warriors of her family. In revenge for the insidious murder of her brothers, she kills the two sons she had with Atli. She serves mead mixed with the blood of the children in goblets fashioned from their skulls, and offers her husband their fried hearts for dinner. Atli is horror-struck when Gudrun tells him the truth following the meal.

While Högni's heart is cut out alive, Gunnar is thrown in chains into the Tower of Snakes. Above the door to the raised passageway we see Gunnar playing a harp with his toes so that the snakes fall asleep, with the exception of one viper, which bites through to his liver, whereupon he too dies.

The entrance wall depicts how Gudrun sets Atli's castle on fire with a torch after stabbing him to death.

Afterwards she tries to find death in the sea, but is saved and carried to the coast beyond. There, she becomes the wife of King Jonakurs.

With this, the end of the saga has not been reached by far. Murder and disaster continue until all of the Nibelungs have perished.

The Singers' Hall

Second only to the throne room, the singers' hall is the most important room in the castle. Ludwig found inspiration for its design in a similar room at Wartburg Castle, in Thuringia. As in that medieval castle, the room here is open to a raised passageway along one length. The room's location under the roof as well as the podium at one end are clearly borrowed from the older castle. This resemblance is certainly not the result of mere imitation. More importantly, Ludwig

August Spieß, design for the mural *Parsifal First Learns about Chivalry*, 1883/84, in the singers' hall

had his castle designed in an apparent effort to achieve historical authenticity as the famous war of the singers is said to have taken place in the early 13th century in the hall at Wartburg Castle. This is also the subject of Wagner's Tannhäuser—an opera which had deeply moved the young prince. And the Minnesang, the glorification of "pure love," is certainly a central iconographical theme throughout the castle. The pictorial representation, however, only takes the art of singing into consideration to a very small degree. The Parsifal legend is of central importance here, and in this regard, the room at Neuschwanstein completely departs from its prototype, which is decorated with images of heroes and saints. Ludwig also elevated this room beyond its function as a room for festivities, to that of a room for worship, fully in keeping with the overall concept of Neuschwanstein.

While the raised passageway tells the past history of the Parsifal saga, Parsifal himself is the subject of the paintings in the singers' hall.

Here the main paintings are described according to the historic concept.

The series of paintings begins on the window side with Parsifal's youth.

Having been raised in rural seclusion, Parsifal sees knights for the first time and, in his child-like simplicity, takes them to be gods.

The inborn desire for action awakes in Parsifal and he takes leave of his mother Herzeloide who, in her wish to see him return soon, sends him off with a poor horse, laughable clothing, and a short spear.

Parsifal arrives at the court of King Arthur who orders him—but only in jest—to fight the red knight, Ither, whom Parsifal kills with his spear, and then takes his armor and his horse.

Parsifal comes to the aid of Queen Condwiramour who is beleaguered by foes, thus winning her hand and her kingdom.

Soon bored of this uneventful, peaceful life, Parsifal again takes to the road and after a long journey meets the ill king Amfortas fishing in a lake, who invites him to the Grail mountain, where he is to be his guest.

Tour of the castle

Singers' hall with a mural depicting the saga of Parsifal

Parsifal is received with hospitality at the Grail mountain and partakes in a feast during which the spear with which Amfortas was wounded and the Grail itself are brought into the hall. Parsifal does not have the courage to ask the question which is expected from him as to the cause of Amfortas' illness, thus destroying all hope that the king will be cured.

After the interrupted meal, Parsifal is taken to a splendid bedroom where pages undress him and maidens serve him sweet wine and fruit.

Parsifal dreams of fierce battles and menacing perils until morning.

As he is leaving the castle of the Grail, a page mocks him for his timidity and calls him a silly goose.

Parsifal is welcomed at King Arthur's round table. During a May feast celebrating the coming of spring, the Grail messenger Kundrie scolds and curses Parsifal for his failure to ask the desired question.

Unaware of having committed a sin, Parsifal doubts in God's righteousness. At odds with himself and the world, he leads a restless life of wandering. On Good Friday he comes to a hermitage where Trevrezent, the brother of Amfortas, lives as a recluse. He takes Parsifal in, who is stiff with cold. Trevrezent learns that he is the knight who visited the Grail mountain and teaches him the secrets of the Grail. Now, reconciled and newly converted, Parsifal leaves the hermit, resolved to once again search for the Grail.

Parisfal meets a heathen knight. After their bitter but un-decided fight, he recognizes in him his half-brother, Feire-fiss, whose face is stained black and white.

Together they travel to the camp of King Arthur's court where a richly bejeweled Kundrie also arrives to ask for-giveness for having defamed Parsifal and to announce that he has been appointed to Amfortas's throne.

After Parsifal returns to his wife Condwiramour and his two young sons Kardeis and Lohengrin, he is met by knights of the Grail, who lead him to the Grail mountain. Through prayer, he delivers Amfortas from his sufferings and is given custody of the Grail.

The cycle finishes with Lohengrin setting off to defend Elsa of Brabant, which at the same time points to the legend of the swan knight.

August Spieß, Parsifal at the Grail Mountain, 1883/84, mural in the singers' hall

The Kitchen

The guided route through the castle ends in the impressive kitchen on the ground floor. Despite the medieval ambiance with the vaulted ceiling supported on sturdy columns, the ovens and cabinets conceal the most modern technology available at the time. In the fireplace stove, for example, the spits are turned by the warmth of the fire. The hot air drives a turbine connected to chains at the side which rotates the spits. The hotter the fire, the faster they rotate. Clever too is the smoke vent for the free-standing stove. Smoke is not drawn upwards, as one might expect, but down through the floor to the heating room, where its warmth can best be put to use.

Many tiled stoves were to be seen in Ludwig's rooms. In addition, the temperature in the castle was

Michael Welter, design for a tiled stove (Ludwig II Museum at Herrenchiemsee)

The kitchen

regulated by a "Calorifère" heating system which could also control air humidity. The warm, humid air was channeled throughout the castle by a system of pipes. Given these technical amenities, it goes without saying that the living quarters in the palace could be supplied with hot and cold running water. There were other technical achievements, often inspired by the latest inventions from the World Exhibition in Paris, such as a dry cell-powered bell system for calling the servants, or a telephone line between the castle

Traditional but Modern

Richard Wenig, Ludwig II on a
Nocturnal Sleigh Ride, c. 1885/86
(Marstallmuseum at Nymphenburg
Palace)

and the administrative building at the foot of the mountain, one of the first telephone systems in Germany.

Traditional but Modern

Anyone who gazes once more at the romantic Lake Alp from the castle would witness a unique spectacle—if Ludwig's most imaginative technical project had been realized, namely a peacock carriage gliding over the lake. The idea was to have a gondola attached to a hydrogen-filled balloon fly 1,240 meters back and forth between Hohenschwangau and the opposite shore. It was to be guided by a connecting cable—a construction which was impossible with the means available at that time. Unfortunately it is not known what the vehicle was to have looked like.

A medical report on Ludwig's state of health mentions this project as proof of the king's allegedly so

Traditional but Modern

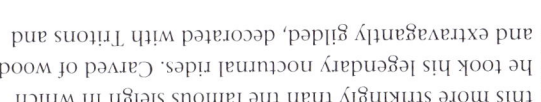

worrying condition, based on a malevolent twisting of this so harmless idea: "... From the realm of uncontrolled fantasy disrespecting all bounds of reality and possibility, comes—as do many other things—his Majesty's fervent wish to fly through the air in a carriage drawn by peacocks ..."

A quotation such as this shows once again how provoking Ludwig's idiosyncratic and autocratic thinking could appear to his contemporaries. This is not the place to speculate about whether Ludwig was in fact mentally ill or not. It is undisputed, however, that Ludwig stood at a political and cultural turning point of historic dimensions, and bore within himself, as well as lived out, all of the tensions of epochal change. No other object connected with the king illustrates this more strikingly than the famous sleigh in which he took his legendary nocturnal rides. Carved of wood and extravagantly gilded, decorated with Tritons and putti bearing the royal insignia before the sleigh, it is to a large extent a copy of a similar vehicle owned by Louis XIV of France. The astounding source of light, which is integrated into the crown, is not a candle, as would be expected, but an electric lightbulb. It was powered by a chromium-based sulphuric acid battery in a leaden sheet metal box hidden under the seat cushion. And most surprising: the lighting system dates from the year 1879, when Edison had just invented the lightbulb! It is likely that this sleigh, which is on exhibit in the Marstall Museum at Nymphenburg Palace, is the first vehicle ever built with electrical illumination.

The connection between old and new only appears as a harmonious synthesis from our modern point of view. The long-outmoded absolutism of Louis XIV from around 1700, and the most modern technological thinking of the bourgeois age as it pushed for democracy, contradicted each other.

Ludwig as the Swan Knight Lohengrin, lithograph by Hans Stuberrauch, Munich

Front cover: Neuschwanstein, view from the north

Back cover: *top left*: Wilhelm Tauber, *Portrait of King Ludwig II in Officer's Uniform*, 1864; *top right*: Ludwig Bierling and Eduard Wollenweber, *Siegfried Slaying the Dragon*, 1885/86, gilded bronze statue in the dining room; *bottom*: the living room

Cartography: Anneli Nau, Munich

© content and layout:
Prestel Verlag, Munich · London · New York, 2000

Photographic credits: all pictures are from the archives held at the Bavarian Administration of State Castles, Palaces, Gardens, and Lakes with the exception of pp. 4/5: Gerold Jung, Ottobrunn; p. 10: photographic archives of the town of Füssen; p. 39: Klaus and Wilhelm Kienberger, Lechbruck; pp. 44/45, 59: Matthias Michel, Erling

The 'Prestel Guide Compact' series, covering Bavaria's castles, palaces, gardens and lakes, is published in cooperation with the Bavarian Administration for State Castles and Palaces and edited by Peter O. Krückmann

Die Deutsche Bibliothek – CIP Einheitsaufnahme data is available
ISBN 3-7913-2368-7

Prestel Verlag
Mandlstrasse 26, 80802 Munich, Germany
Tel. (089) 38 17 09 - 0, fax (089) 38 17 09 -35;
4 Bloomsbury Place, London WC1A 2QA
Tel. (020) 7323 5004, fax (020) 7636 8004;
175 Fifth Avenue, New York, NY 10010
Tel. (212) 995-2720, fax (212) 995-2733

Prestel books are available worldwide. Please contact your nearest bookseller or write to any of the above addresses for information concerning your local distributor.

Translated from the German by Jacqueline Guigui-Stolberg
Edited by Christopher Wynne
Designed and typeset by Norbert Dinkel, Munich
Lithography by ReproLine, Munich
Printed by Peradruck, Gräfelfing
Bound by Attenberger, Munich

Printed in Germany on acid-free paper
ISBN 3-7913-2368-7

The cross in Lake Starnberg to commemorate the death of Ludwig II

As the highest representative of his state, Ludwig could not, in the long run, maintain his self-absorbed life-style, with all its implications, as the only valid norm. His downfall was a foregone conclusion. Only since Ludwig II and his unresolved death in Lake Starnberg have gone down in history, can his creations—above all his three most important building projects, Neuschwanstein, Linderhof, and Herrenchiemsee—be experienced as the serene, fairy-tale world of a fairytale king, who was completely out of touch with reality.